A MIDSUMMER NIGHT'S DREAM

Adapted and abridged by Andrew Biliter

Based on the play
by William Shakespeare

WANT TO PERFORM THIS PLAY? YOU NEED TO GET THE RIGHTS!

But don't worry, it's easy. We have affordable licensing options for any size organization, and we'll get your contract finalized in just a few days.

Questions?
info@lighthouseplays.com
(872) 228-7826
lighthouseplays.com

CAST OF CHARACTERS

The Royal Court of Athens
THESEUS, King of Athens
HIPPOLYTA the Amazon, future Queen of Athens
EGEUS, a courtier, father of Hermia
PHILOSTRATE to Theseus

The Lovers
HELENA, a young noblewoman, in love with Lysander
LYSANDER, a young nobleman, in love with Helena
DEMETRIUS, a young nobleman, in love with Helena
HERMIA, a young noblewoman, in love with Demetrius

The Rude Mechanicals, a troupe of amateur actors
NICK BOTTOM, the weaver (plays Pyramus)
PETER QUINCE, the carpenter
FRANCIS FLUTE, the bellows-maker (plays Thisbe)
ROBIN STARVELING, the tailor (plays Moonshine)
TOM SNOUT, the tinker (plays Wall)
SNUG the Joiner (plays Lion)

The Fairy Court
OBERON, King of the Fairies
PUCK, his servant
TITANIA, Queen of the Fairies
Fairies attending on Titania:
PEASEBLOSSOM
COBWEB
MOTE
MUSTARDSEED

ACT 1, SCENE 1

Athens. The palace of THESEUS.

Enter THESEUS, HIPPOLYTA, PHILOSTRATE, and Attendants.

THESEUS
Come, fair Hippolyta, our wedding day
Is close at hand. Just four more days until
The new moon comes, and we can say, "I do."

HIPPOLYTA
Four days will quickly steep themselves in night.
Four nights will quickly dream away the time.
And then the moon will be a silver bow,
New-bent to launch us into wedded bliss.

PHILOSTRATE
King Theseus!

THESEUS
Here comes the Philostrate.
Good Philostrate, have you prepared our vows?

PHILOSTRATE
My lord, I fear I'm stuck. The problem is,
You've never told me how you came to meet.

THESEUS
Hippolyta?

HIPPOLYTA
He wooed me with his sword.

PHILOSTRATE
Now what exactly do you mean by that?

HIPPOLYTA
Well, I was Queen of Amazonia.

THESEUS
And then I conquered Amazonia.

HIPPOLYTA
And then love... conquered both of us.

PHILOSTRATE
I see. Then you're his captive…

THESEUS
And I hers.

PHILOSTRATE
Oh, good. So there were no hard feelings in the end.

> *THESEUS and HIPPOLYTA are staring into each other's eyes.*
> *It's awkward for PHILOSTRATE.*

PHILOSTRATE
Well, I think I've got enough to work with now.

> *Exit PHILOSTRATE.*

> *Enter EGEUS, HERMIA, LYSANDER, and DEMETRIUS.*

EGEUS
Hooray for Theseus, our beloved duke!

THESEUS
Good Egeus, thanks! And how are things with you?

EGEUS
Most wretched, I'm afraid. I've come to gripe.

THESEUS
What grieves you?

EGEUS
It's my daughter, Hermia.
Stand forth, Demetrius. My noble lord,
This man has my consent to marry her.
But he can't, because — stand forth, Lysander —
This man's bewitched the bosom of my child.
You! You, Lysander! You have given her rhymes,
And interchanged love tokens with my child.
You have, by moonlight, at her window, sung,
Read poems to her in a husky voice,
Seduced her with bracelets, rings, gawds, conceits,
Knacks, trifles, nosegays, sweetmeats! Stole her heart,
And turned obedience to hateful spite.

THESEUS
I see.

EGEUS
A girl must marry as her father chooses!
And since she is refusing to obey,
I beg the ancient privilege of Athens,
That I dispose of her as I see fit,
To him… or to her death, as law dictates.

THESEUS
What say you, Hermia? Be advised, dear child:
Your father gave you life; that's no small thing.
You should respect his judgment, and besides,
Demetrius is a worthy gentleman.

HERMIA
So is Lysander.

THESEUS
Yes, but I would say
Your father's wishes tip the scale a bit.
Do as he asks you.

HERMIA
Pardon me, your grace,
But what's the penalty if I refuse?

THESEUS
You'll die. Or—you can go live as a nun.

HERMIA
A nun it is, then.

HIPPOLYTA
Truly? That's your choice?
To be a barren sister all your life,
Chanting faint hymns to the cold, fruitless moon?

HERMIA (*indicating DEMETRIUS*)
I'd rather wear a habit than his yoke.

DEMETRIUS
Come now, sweet Hermia. I'm not so bad.
Lysander, do what's right and give her up.

LYSANDER
You have her father's love, Demetrius;
Let me have Hermia's. You can marry him!

EGEUS
Scornful Lysander! Yes, I like him best,
And now I see how right my judgment was.

LYSANDER
Sir, inform me. What is it I lack?
Demetrius is of no higher rank,
Likewise our fortunes are about the same,
The only difference is, I love her more.
And more importantly, she loves me back!
Demetrius, meanwhile, lives to play the field.
He trifled with our dear friend, Helena.
He wooed her, reeled her in, and won her heart,
Then spurned her in a manner most abrupt.
And to this day she dotes on him, poor girl.

THESEUS
I've heard this tale. You're that Demetrius?
Your name precedes you, not in a good way.
My judgment in this case remains the same,
But you and I are going to have a chat;
Responsibility will be the theme.
So Hermia, to review, your choices are:
Death, nunnery, marry Demetrius.
You have until my wedding to decide.
That's four days. Come, Hippolyta, my love.
Demetrius, Egeus, you come, too.

EGEUS
With duty and desire we follow you.

Exeunt all but LYSANDER and HERMIA.

She runs to him and weeps.

LYSANDER
There, there, my darling. You know what they say:
The course of true love never did run smooth.
We're not the first to suffer, nor the last.

HERMIA
I shall cry harder, then, and shed one tear
For every star-crossed lover in the world!

LYSANDER
No, darling, listen now. I have a plan.

HERMIA
What is it, then?

LYSANDER
Let's run away.

HERMIA
To where?

LYSANDER
We'll go live at my aunt's house by the sea.
It's twenty miles away, beyond the woods,
Beyond the bounds of cruel Athenian law.
So we'd be free to marry as we choose.
What do you say?

HERMIA
Oh, dear Lysander! Yes!

LYSANDER
Now, here is what we'll do. Tomorrow night,
You're going to sneak out of your father's house,
And in the wood, a mile outside the town,
I will be waiting by the hollow tree.

HERMIA
By all the fireflies that light the air,
I promise you, my love, I will be there.

LYSANDER
So it's agreed. Look, here comes Helena!

Enter HELENA.

HERMIA
Why, Helena! You're looking well today.

HELENA
Ugh. No I'm not, but thank you anyway.
Quite honestly, I wish I looked like you.

HERMIA
Now, don't say that.

HELENA
Why shouldn't I? It's true.
Your face is all Demetrius can see.
Oh, what I'd give to have him gaze at me!
Please, teach me how you look, and with what art
You sway the motion of Demetrius' heart!

HERMIA
I frown at him, and yet he loves me still.

HELENA
I wish your frowns could teach my smiles that skill.

HERMIA
The more I hate, the more he follows me.

HELENA
The more I love, the more he dodges me.

HERMIA
Well, he's a fool. Is that some fault of mine?

HELENA
Your fault's your beauty. I wish it were mine.

HERMIA
Take comfort; he will no more see my face.

HELENA
How do you mean?

HERMIA (*taking LYSANDER's hand*)
We're going to flee this place.

HELENA
How?

HERMIA
Should we tell her how?

LYSANDER
I think we should.
Tomorrow night. We meet up in the wood.

HERMIA
Around the spot where you and I once played.
And from there, he and I will run away
And leave this town for good. Farewell, sweet friend.
I hope you will find happiness in the end!

Exit HERMIA and LYSANDER.

HELENA
Ugh! They're so happy! Why can't that be me?
Our friends say I am just as fair as she.
But I care only what Demetrius thinks,
And in his eyes, my valuation sinks
Lower and lower with every passing day.
And—hold on, wait. Now, here's a clever thought!
I'll tell Demetrius about their plot.
Then run off in pursuit of them will he,
And in the process, pay some heed to me!
I s'pose it's not the most ingenious plan,
But I'll do anything to get that man.

Exit.

ACT 1, SCENE 2

Athens. Behind the home of PETER QUINCE.

Enter the Actors: QUINCE, SNUG, BOTTOM, FLUTE, SNOUT, and STARVELING. They are doing their warm-ups.

QUINCE
All right, all right! Quiet down. Now, is all our company here?

BOTTOM
I think it's best you call out all the names simultaneously, one at a time.

QUINCE
My thoughts exactly. Here is a scroll with the names of all the men in Athens who are fit to take part in a short play, to be performed for the duke and duchess on their wedding night. Answer as I call you.

BOTTOM
Peter Quince, it sits to reason that you should first tell what the play treats on, then read the names of the actors.

QUINCE
Right. Our play is "The Most Lamentable Comedy and Most Cruel Death of Pyramus and Thisbe."

BOTTOM
A very good piece of work, I assure you. Plus it's funny. Now, good Peter Quince, call forth your actors by the scroll. Masters, spread out.

They spread out.

QUINCE
He means gather round.

They gather round.

QUINCE
All right. Nick Bottom, the weaver.

BOTTOM
Ready. Name what part I am for, and proceed.

QUINCE
You, Nick Bottom, are set down for Pyramus.

BOTTOM
What is Pyramus? A lover, or a tyrant?

QUINCE
A lover, who kills himself most gallantly for love.

BOTTOM
The part will require me to shed real tears. Fortunately, that is a skill I have practiced. By the end, I'll have audience weeping inconceivably. Go on to the next name.

QUINCE
Francis—

BOTTOM
As an actor, though, my specialty is tyrants. Not that I want to be typeset or anything, but listen:
The raging rocks
And shivering shocks
Shall break the locks
Of prison gates;
And Fibbus's car
Shall shine from far
And make and mar
The foolish Fates.

The other Actors applaud.

BOTTOM
This was lofty. Now do the rest.

QUINCE
Francis Flute, the bellows-mender.

FLUTE
Here, Peter Quince.

QUINCE
Flute, you will play the part of Thisbe.

FLUTE
What is Thisbe? A wandering knight?

QUINCE
It is the lady that Pyramus must love.

FLUTE
Oh, please don't make me play a woman! I have a beard coming.

Everyone scrutinizes his face for traces of a beard. There are none.

QUINCE
I think it will be all right as long as you speak in a very high voice and wear the wig.
Do we have the wig for him? Good.

BOTTOM
What if you had me hide my face, and then I could play both Pyramus and Thisbe;
one in a deep voice, and the other in a palmetto.
(*In a low voice*) "Thisbe? Thisbe, dear, where are you?"
(*In a high voice*) "Pyramus, Pyramus, it is I, thy Thisne dear, thy lady dear!"

FLUTE
Does that mean he gets to take my part?

QUINCE
No. He is not taking anyone's part! Bottom must play Pyramus. Flute, you will play
Thisbe.

BOTTOM
Fine. Proceed.

QUINCE
Robin Starveling, the tailor.

STARVELING
Here, Peter Quince.

QUINCE
Robin Starveling, you must play Thisbe's mother.

STARVELING (*pumping his fist*)
Yes!

QUINCE
Tom Snout, the tinker.

SNOUT
Here, Peter Quince.

QUINCE
You, Pyramus' father.

SNOUT
Got it.

QUINCE
Myself; Thisbe's father. Snug, the joiner.

SNUG
Here.

QUINCE
You, the lion's part. And that, I believe, is everybody.

SNUG
Do you have the lion's part written? If it is, I pray you, give it to me now, for I
am slow of study.

QUINCE
You won't need a script. The lion's part is all ad lib. He just roars.

BOTTOM
Ooh! Let me play the lion, too! And I will roar so well that the duke will say,
"Let him roar again, let him roar again."

QUINCE
Yes, and you'd roar so well that it would terrify the duchess and the ladies, and
then we'd all be hanged.

SNOUT
It's true.

BOTTOM
Then I'll roar gently.

QUINCE
No, Bottom. You can play no part but Pyramus; for Pyramus is a
sweet-faced man; a proper man, as one might see on a summer's day; a most
lovely gentleman-like man: therefore you must play Pyramus.

BOTTOM
Well, I shall. What kind of beard should I wear?

QUINCE
Whatever kind of beard you want.

BOTTOM
I'm thinking either a straw-colored beard or an orange, tawny-colored beard.

QUINCE
Excellent.

BOTTOM
But I could also appear clean-shaven, as the French do.

QUINCE
Masters, here are your parts. And it is my pleading request, my strong desire, that you memorize them by to-morrow night, and meet me in the palace wood, a mile outside of town, by moonlight. There will we rehearse. Our play is a surprise, so keep a lid on and be sure you are not followed. Fail me not!

BOTTOM
We will meet; and there we may rehearse most obscenely and courageously! Adieu.

Exeunt.

ACT 2, SCENE 1

A wood near Athens.

Enter FAIRY and PUCK.

PUCK
How now, spirit! Whither wander you?

FAIRY
Over hill, over dale,
Through the bush, through the briar,
Over park, over pale,
Through the flood, through the fire,
I do wander everywhere,
Swifter than the moon's sphere;
And I serve the fairy queen,
To dew her orbs upon the green.

PUCK
The king will hold his revels here tonight,
Take care the queen come not within his sight.
For Oberon is in a jealous rage.

FAIRY
Why so?

PUCK
Because he wants the queen's new page,
A child she kidnapped from an Indian king.
She's never had so sweet a changeling.
But Oberon thinks he should have the child,
To roam about with him in forests wild.
The queen, of course, will not give up the boy,
But crowns him with flowers and makes him all her joy.
And now they never meet in grove or green,
By fountain clear, or spangled starlight sheen
Without a fight! They spar so loud, the elves
Creep into acorn cups and hide themselves.

FAIRY
Either I mistake your shape and making quite,
Or else you are that shrewd and naughty sprite?
The one called Puck?

PUCK
You've got that right.
I am that merry wanderer of the night.

FAIRY
Who frights the maidens of the villagery,
And makes sure travelers lose their way?

PUCK
That's me.
But look out, fairy! Here comes Oberon.

FAIRY
And here's Titania. We had best be gone!

> *Enter, from one side, OBERON; from the other, TITANIA, with her FAIRIES.*

OBERON
Ill met by moonlight, proud Titania.

TITANIA
Indeed, jealous Oberon! Very ill-timed.
Fairies, let's go. He's not getting any of this.

OBERON
Is that any way to talk to your lord?

TITANIA
Well, if you're my lord then I must be your lady. But if I'm your lady, then tell me, who was the shepherdess you were playing your panpipes for yesterday?

OBERON
Audrey and I are friends and that is all.

TITANIA
And before that you were in India doing God knows what.
Did you come back to see Hippolyta, your bouncing Amazon?
You must have been crushed to learn she was engaged.

OBERON
That takes some nerve, Titania, bringing up Hippolyta when I know how you feel about Theseus. It's you who's feeling crushed, because it was you who led him astray from all those other women: Aegles, Ariadne, Antopia. That's just the A's, I could go on.

TITANIA
You really get inventive when you're jealous. Perhaps you should spend more of that energy doing your job.

OBERON
I'm a god!

TITANIA
Then act like one. Look around you, husband. Since midsummer, the girls and I have never, never made it all the way through a dance without you butting in. No matter where we go, be it hill, dale, rushy brook or forest glen, there you are with your sidekick, sabotaging us. And I know you know that we don't dance for sport. We dance to please the winds. So when we couldn't dance for them, the winds grew vengeful. They sucked contagious fogs out of the sea, and these were soon unleashed upon the land, making it rain nonstop. Now the rivers are flooded, the fields are filled with mud, animals are dying, and the forest has grown wild. I'm not even sure we'll be able to have seasons this year, and the sad part is, it's all because of us. This petty quarrel has gone on too long.

OBERON
But I know a way to end it.

TITANIA
How?

OBERON
By giving me what I want. All I'm asking for is one boy to be my henchman.

TITANIA
Never!

OBERON
How long will you be staying in this wood?

TITANIA
Perhaps until Theseus' wedding day. If you'll come dance with us, we won't object. If not, avoid me, and I'll do the same.

OBERON
Give me the boy and I will go with you.

TITANIA
Not for your Fairy Kingdom! Fairies, away.
I'm worried I may punch him if I stay.

Exeunt TITANIA and FAIRIES.

OBERON
That's right, go on! But don't kid yourself into thinking that you've won! My
gentle Puck, come sit. Do remember that time when we were sitting on a
promontory, and we looked and saw a mermaid on a dolphin's back, and she
sang to us in a voice so lovely that it made the seas calm, and caused certain
stars in the sky to explode?

PUCK
I remember.

OBERON
Well, at that very moment I looked up, and saw something that you could not
see, flying between the cold moon and the earth. Can you guess what it was?

PUCK
Space dust?

OBERON
Cupid.

PUCK
Cupid! Was he armed?

OBERON
He was. In fact he was letting loose his love-shaft at that very moment.

PUCK
Who was he firing at?

OBERON
Queen Elizabeth the First. It doesn't matter, though. He missed. The point is, I
marked where the arrow fell. It fell upon a little western flower, once white,
now purple from love's wound. Fetch me that flower. The juice of it, when laid
on sleeping eyelids, will make any man or woman madly dote upon the next
living creature that they see. Fetch me that herb right now and don't delay.

PUCK
I'll put a girdle round about the earth in forty minutes.

OBERON
Once the herb is mine, I'll use it on Titania while she sleeps. This should be fun.
(*He hears noises offstage.*) But who's that there? I am invisible, and will overhear
their conference.

Enter DEMETRIUS and HELENA, following him.

DEMETRIUS
I love you not, why can't you let me be?
Where are Lysander and fair Hermia?
You told me they had gone into this wood!
But here I am and all I see are trees.
You are a sadness. Follow me no more!

HELENA
You stab me, but my heart is true as steel.
And you are the magnet that draws me in.

DEMETRIUS
But what's the draw? I'm never kind to you.
How many ways are there to say "Get lost?"
I do not, cannot, will not love you, ever.

HELENA
You saying that just makes me love you more.
Don't be afraid to treat me as you will.
Neglect me, use me, spurn me, strike me, love.
Just give me leave, unworthy as I am,
To follow you. Can you at least do that?

DEMETRIUS
It makes me sick to look at you sometimes.

HELENA
And I feel sick if I don't look at you.

DEMETRIUS
I'll run from you! I'll hide me in the wood.
And leave you to the mercy of wild beasts.

HELENA
No, you're the beast, and I the hunter, love!
Apollo flies, and Daphne holds the chase!

DEMETRIUS
I will not stand for this. Please! Let me go!
And if you choose to follow, mark my words:
I will do you mischief in the wood!

HELENA
Ay, in the temple, in the town, the field, you do me mischief. Fie, Demetrius!

Exit DEMETRIUS.

HELENA
I'll follow you and make a heaven of hell,
To die upon the hand I love so well.

Exit HELENA.

OBERON
What a woman!
Nymph, before this night is through,
I'll see to it that he is chasing you.
And that's a promise.

PUCK
Here's the flower!

OBERON
Good. Now with its juice I'll streak Titania's eyes.
And make her full of hateful fantasies.
You take some, too. Look here, my gentle dove:
A sweet Athenian lady is in love
With a disdainful youth. Anoint his eyes;
And do it so the next thing that he spies
Will be the lady. You will know this John
By the Athenian garments he has on.
And use it liberally; get right in there,
I'll have him love her more than she can bear.
Return to me before the first cock crow!

PUCK
Fear not, my lord. Your servant shall do so.

Exeunt.

ACT 2, SCENE 2

Another part of the wood.

Enter TITANIA, with her FAIRIES.

TITANIA
Come, ladies! Lull me with a fairy song;
Then to your offices and let me rest.

FAIRIES
You spotted snakes with double tongue,
Thorny hedgehogs, be not seen;
Newts and blind-worms, do no wrong,
Come not near our fairy queen.
Philomel, with melody
Sing in our sweet lullaby;
Lulla, lulla, lullaby, lulla, lulla, lullaby:
Weaving spiders, come not here;
Shoo, you long-legged spinners, hence!
Beetles black, approach not near;
Worm nor snail, do no offense.
Philomel, with melody,
Sing in our sweet lullaby;
Lulla, lulla, lullaby, lulla, lulla, lullaby.

TITANIA yawns and goes to sleep.

MUSTARDSEED
Shhh! Away! Now all is well.

PEASEBLOSSOM
Wait. One of us stand sentinel. (*She chooses COBWEB.*) You.

Exeunt FAIRIES, except for COBWEB. TITANIA sleeps.

*Enter OBERON from behind. He puts COBWEB to sleep with the
flower's aroma and approaches TITANIA.*

OBERON (*while administering the juice*)
What you see when you awake,
For your true love you shall take.
Be it mouse, or cat, or bear,
Goat, or boar with bristled hair,

In your eye that first appears
When you wake, make it your dear.
(*pause*)
Wake when something vile is near.

Exit.

Enter LYSANDER and HERMIA.

LYSANDER
My love, you're faint from wandering this wood!
Plus, honestly, I think I've lost our way.
Let's rest now, Hermia. Does that sound good?
These woods look better in the light of day.

HERMIA
All right, Lysander. Make yourself a bed;
This mossy bank is where I'll lay my head.

LYSANDER
One turf can serve as pillow for us both;
One heart, one bed, two bosoms and one oath.

HERMIA
No, good Lysander, that is much too near.
Go lie a little further off, my dear.

LYSANDER
Oh, Hermia, please! That isn't what I meant.
My motives are entirely innocent!
I only want to share this bank with you.
No funny stuff, I promise, love. It's true!

HERMIA
I'm sure it is, Lysander. Even so,
For modesty's sake, I'm begging you to go.
Just over there. Thaaaat's right. Goodnight, sweet friend.
Now let us dream of love that never ends.

LYSANDER
Amen to that! I'll sleep now feeling glad.
And you were right. This bed is not so bad.

They sleep.

Enter PUCK.

PUCK
Through the forest have I gone.
But Athenian found I none.
Night and silence… Who is there?
Weeds of Athens does he wear:
He's the one my master spied,
Whose cruelty made a poor girl cry.
And here's the maiden! Sleeping sound,
On the dank and dirty ground.
Pretty soul! She should not lie
Near such an undeserving guy.
Snake, into your eyes I hurl
A charm to make you love that girl.
So awake when I am gone.
For I must now to Oberon.

   Exit.

   Enter DEMETRIUS and HELENA, running.

HELENA
You run so fast, my sweet Demetrius!

DEMETRIUS
Leave me alone, and do not haunt me thus!

HELENA
Don't leave me now! It's dark. I could get lost.

DEMETRIUS
Oh, losing you is clearly worth the cost!

   Exit.

HELENA
O, I am out of breath in this fond chase!
What makes him hate me so? Is it my face?
It must be. I'm as ugly as a bear;
No wonder poor Demetrius was scared.
But who is here? Lysander, on the ground!
What, dead? Asleep? No blood here to be found.
Lysander, if you live, good sir, awake!

LYSANDER (*awaking*)
And run through fire I will, for your sweet sake!

You are so beautiful that I could die.
And where's Demetrius? I want to kill that guy.

HELENA
Lysander, what has gotten into you?
You'd kill him? Why? For loving Hermia, too?
Fair Hermia loves you best, so be content.

LYSANDER
Content with Hermia! No, I do repent
The tedious minutes I with her have spent.
Not Hermia but Helena I love:
Who wouldn't change a raven for a dove?

HELENA
You mock me! Ugh! What is it with you men?

Exit.

LYSANDER
I guess she didn't notice Hermia, then.
And henceforth, nor will I. Who needs her, right?
My job's to honor Helen and be her knight!

Exit.

HERMIA (*awaking*)
Help me, Lysander, help me! Do your best
To pull this crawling serpent from my chest!
Ay me, for pity! What a dream was here!
Lysander, look how I do quake with fear.
I dreamed a serpent ate my heart away,
And you sat smiling at his cruel prey.
Lysander? Are you there? Lysander, dear!
What, out of earshot? Gone? You were just here.
Well, this is scary. What am I to do?
I'll either die out here or I'll find you.

Exit.

ACT 3, SCENE 1

The wood. TITANIA lies asleep.

*Enter QUINCE, SNUG, BOTTOM, FLUTE, SNOUT,
and STARVELING.*

BOTTOM
Are we all here?

QUINCE
All here and all on time. And what a convenient spot for our rehearsal. This mossy patch will be our stage, and that bush is the dressing room. Let's take it from the top.

BOTTOM
Peter Quince.

QUINCE
What is it, dear Bottom?

BOTTOM
There are things in this comedy of Pyramus and Thisbe that will never please. First, Pyramus must draw a sword and kill himself. The ladies in the audience cannot abide this.

SNOUT
Ooh, he's right. I hadn't thought of that!

STARVELING
I believe we'll have to leave the killing out, when all is done.

BOTTOM
Hold on. I have a device to make it work. Write me a prologue, and let the prologue say, basically, that we will do no harm with our swords, and that Pyramus does not actually die. And then, just to be on the safe side, say that I am not actually Pyramus at all, but Bottom the weaver.

STARVELING
I like it.

FLUTE
I think it will put people at ease.

QUINCE
All right, then, we'll add a prologue. So I guess I'm writing that.

SNOUT
And will not the ladies be afeared of the lion?

STARVELING
Yes, that concerns me, too.

FLUTE
I'm afeared of them myself.

BOTTOM
And rightly so! Lions, when they are alive, are the most dangerous waterfowl known to man.

SNOUT
So that does it. We need a second prologue to tell that he is not a lion.

BOTTOM
Or we could just have the lion come out, pull down his mask, and say something to the defect of, "Fair Ladies: Fear not. Tremble not at the sight of me. If you think I come here as a lion, I am sorry. I am no such thing. I am a man like any other." And here you could even say it plainly, "My name is Snug the joiner."

SNUG
But you said all I had to do was roar.

QUINCE
All right, that should work. But this still leaves two hard things. First, the play calls for Pyramus and Thisbe to meet by moonlight, but we'll be performing indoors.

SNOUT
We could leave the windows open and let the moon shine in!

BOTTOM
There's a thought.

QUINCE
Or, we could have one of us come in holding a lantern and say that he represents the person of Moonshine.

ALL
Oooh.

STARVELING
Very abstract. I like it.

QUINCE
The other problem is we must have a wall on stage, because the script has
Pyramus and Thisbe talking through a chink in the wall. Thoughts?

SNOUT
Hmm. You can never bring in a wall. What say you, Bottom?

BOTTOM
Someone will have to play the wall.

FLUTE
But how?

BOTTOM
In the one hand he'll hold a chunk of plaster, to signify wall, and with his other,
he will hold his fingers thus, and through that cranny Pyramus and Thisbe shall
whisper.

QUINCE
Done. Come, sit down, all of you, and let's rehearse. Pyramus, you enter from
over there.

PUCK
What hempen home-spuns have we swaggering here,
So near the cradle of the fairy queen?
What's this? A play? A spectator I'll be.
An actor, too, perhaps, if I see cause.

QUINCE
Speak, Pyramus. Thisbe, stand forth.

BOTTOM
Thisbe, thy breath hath the sweet odious of flowers—

QUINCE
Odors! Odors!

BOTTOM.
Sweet odors of flowers.
But hark, a voice! Stay thou but here awhile,
And by and by I will to thee appear.

    Exit.

PUCK
He's like no Pyramus I've seen before.

FLUTE
Must I speak now?

QUINCE
Yes! You must.

FLUTE
Most radiant Pyramus,
As true as truest horse that never tires,
I'll meet thee, love, at Ninny's tomb.

QUINCE
It's "Ninus' tomb," man! And you must wait for Pyramus to come back to say
that! You can't just say it to no one.

FLUTE
Oh, Pyramus, come to thy Thisbe fair!

Re-enter PUCK, and BOTTOM with a donkey's head.

BOTTOM
Here I am! See? I wasn't gone a hair!

QUINCE
O monstrous! O strange! We are haunted. Pray, masters! Fly, masters! Help!

Exeunt QUINCE, SNUG, FLUTE, SNOUT, and STARVELING.

PUCK
Haha! I'll follow you! I'll lead you all around!
Through bog, through bush, through brake, through brier.
Sometimes a horse I'll be, sometime a hound,
A hog, a headless bear, or sometime… FIRE!

Exit.

BOTTOM
Why do they run away? This is a trick to make me feel afeard. Hey, you!

Re-enter SNOUT.

SNOUT
O Bottom, bless you, you are changed! You are… translated!

Exit SNOUT.

BOTTOM
I see what they're up to. They're trying to make an ass of me. Well, I'll show them. I will not leave this spot. And I will walk up and down and I will sing so they hear me. I'm not afraid.
(*sings*)
O, THE OUSEL COCK SO BLACK OF HUE,
WITH ORANGE-TAWNY BILL,
THE THROSTLE WITH HIS NOTE SO TRUE,
THE WREN WITH LITTLE QUILL

TITANIA (*awaking*)
What angel wakes me from my flowery bed?

BOTTOM (*sings*)
THE FINCH, THE SPARROW AND THE LARK,
THE PLAIN-SONG CUCKOO GRAY,
WHOSE NOTE FULL MANY A MAN DOTH MARK,
AND DARES NOT ANSWER NAY —

TITANIA
I pray you, gentle mortal, sing again.
My ear is much enamored of your song,
As is my eye enthralled by your shape.
Indeed your manly, rugged virtues move me
At first view to declare—nay, swear—I love thee.

BOTTOM
Methinks, mistress, you should have little reason to love me. And yet, one must admit that reason and love are rarely seen together nowadays.

TITANIA (*laughs flirtatiously*)
You are as wise as you are beautiful.

BOTTOM
I am not so wise as all that. I don't even know how to get out of this wood.

TITANIA
Out of this wood do not desire to go.
You shall remain here, whether you will or no.
For I do love you: therefore, go with me;
I'll give you fairies to attend you, see?

And they shall fetch you jewels from the deep,
And sing to you while you do fall asleep.
Peaseblossom, Cobweb, Mote and Mustardseed!

The FAIRIES approach.

PEASEBLOSSOM
Ready.

COBWEB
And I.

MOTE
And I.

MUSTARDSEED
And I.

ALL
Where shall we go?

TITANIA
Be kind and courteous to this gentleman. Greet him.

PEASEBLOSSOM
Hail, mortal!

COBWEB
Hail!

MOTE
Hail!

MUSTARDSEED
Hail!

BOTTOM
Pleased to make your acquaintances! And you, good sir, I beseech your name!

TITANIA
Answer, and tell what courtesies you will do him.

PEASEBLOSSOM
Peaseblossom. I'll feed you apricots and dewberries,
with purple grapes, green figs, and mulberries.

BOTTOM
That sounds like good feasting! Master Peaseblossom, I shall desire more of your acquaintance. And your name, sir?

MOTE
Mote. I'll steal the honey bags from humble-bees, and make sure there's always honey in your tea.

BOTTOM
I love the sweet life! Thanks, Master Mote. And your name, honest gentleman?

MUSTARDSEED
I'm Mustardseed. I'll pluck the wings from painted butterflies to fan the moonbeams from your sleeping eyes.

BOTTOM
How lyrical! Thanks, good Master Mustardseed. I should like more of your acquaintance, too! And last but not least?

COBWEB
Cobweb. If you cut your finger, I'll wrap it so it doesn't bleed.

BOTTOM
A very kind offer, Doctor Cobweb. If that happens, I'll come to you.

TITANIA
I'll to my bower; lead my love to me.

BOTTOM snorts and hee-haws as the fairies tickle him.

TITANIA
And tie his tongue up. Bring him silently.

Exeunt.

ACT 3, SCENE 2

The wood.

Enter OBERON.

OBERON
I wonder if Titania is awake. And if she is, I wonder what she saw. If only I had a messenger to tell me these things.

Enter PUCK.

PUCK
Master—

OBERON
Ah, here he is! How now, mad spirit? What havoc have you wreaked here in the grove?

PUCK
My mistress with a monster is in love!
It happened in that dull and sleepy hour,
When she lay sleeping in her bed of flowers.
A crew of dunces, rude mechanicals,
Who work for bread in the Athenian stalls,
Had come together to rehearse a play
Intended for great Theseus' wedding day.
The shallowest thick-skin of this barren sort,
Was he that played Pyramus in their sport.
Well, as soon as he stepped off their patch of grass,
I did replace his head with that of an ass.
And when his fellows saw him they did fly!
Like wild geese who've caught the hunter's eye.
I led them on in this distracted fear
And left sweet Pyramus transfigured there.
When in that moment so it came to pass
That Titania waked, and straightway loved and ass!

OBERON
This far exceeds my wildest expectations. And what of our Athenian? Did you squeeze the love juice in his eyes?

PUCK
I did. And with the woman by his side,
So when he wakes, she won't escape his sight!

Enter DEMETRIUS and HERMIA.

OBERON
Stand close. This is the same Athenian.

PUCK
This is the woman, but not this the man…

DEMETRIUS
O Venus fair, why do you spurn me so?
I only wish to bask here in your glow.

HERMIA
Just tell me where his body is, you creep!

DEMETRIUS
Whose?

HERMIA
Lysander's. You killed him in his sleep.

DEMETRIUS
I know not where he is, nor do I care.
But I am not a murderer, I swear!

HERMIA
If he's alive, then find him. Make the rounds.

DEMETRIUS
I'd sooner give his carcass to my hounds!

HERMIA
So you admit you killed him, then.

DEMETRIUS
Oh, hell!

HERMIA
If not, then prove to me that he is well.

DEMETRIUS
And for that comfort, what would I obtain?

HERMIA
The privilege not to see my face again!
So long, Demetrius. I hope you drown.

Exit HERMIA.

DEMETRIUS
I guess I'd better wait till she cools down,
(*yawns*) And while I'm at it, get some sleep tonight;
For worries seem less heavy when it's light.

He sleeps.

OBERON
Puck.

PUCK
I goofed.

OBERON
It would appear that way.
You'll fix this. Find Helena and bring her near.
I'll get Demetrius ready over here.

PUCK
I go, I go. Look how I go,
Swifter than an arrow from Cupid's bow!

OBERON (*applying the juice*)
Flower of this purple dye,
Sink in apple of his eye.

Re-enter PUCK.

PUCK
Captain of our fairy band,
Helena is here at hand!
And so's the youth!

OBERON
The noise they make
Will cause Demetrius to awake!

Enter HELENA, pursued by LYSANDER.

LYSANDER
Why would you think I'm joking when I woo?
(*points to his tears*) See? When I vow, I weep. That means it's true!

HELENA
You told me you loved Hermia. You swore!
Ay me, do words mean nothing anymore?

LYSANDER
I had no judgment when I made that vow!

HELENA
What makes you think that you have judgment now?

DEMETRIUS (*waking*)
O Helena, goddess, nymph, perfect, divine!
To what shall I compare your eyes so fine?
Crystal is muddy. Oh, but let me kiss
This dainty little hand, this seal of bliss!

HELENA
O spite. O hell! I see, you all are bent
To set against me for your merriment.
You vow, and swear, and super-praise my parts,
When I am sure you hate me with your hearts.
If you were men, as men you are in show,
You would not use a gentle lady so!

LYSANDER
You are unkind, Demetrius. Be not so.
For you love Hermia. This you know I know.
So good! I want no place in Hermia's heart,
You can have her, and I can have your part.

DEMETRIUS
Lysander, keep your Hermia. I want none.
I may have loved her once, but now we're done.
My heart just took a day trip over there,
And now it has returned to Helen fair,
Remaining always.

LYSANDER
Helen, he is mad!

DEMETRIUS
Don't question things you do not understand!

HELENA
A lot of work has gone into this prank.

Enter HERMIA.

HERMIA
Lysander, love! (*She embraces him.*) You left me by the bank.
Can you explain why you did treat me so?

LYSANDER
I fell in love. And then I had to go.

HERMIA
What love could have removed me from your sight?

LYSANDER
Fair Helena, whose fire lights the night.
Why seek me out? My absence was your cue
That I no longer care a whit for you.

HERMIA
You speak not as you think. It cannot be.

HELENA
Oh! So you are part of this conspiracy!
Now I perceive you have conjoined all three
To fashion this false sport in spite of me!
Injurious Hermia. Most ungrateful maid!
Is all the counsel that we two have shared,
The sisters' vows, the hours that we have spent,
Our schoolyard days, is all of that forgot?
For what? To join with these malicious men
In scorning me, your poor, devoted friend?

HERMIA
I understand not what you mean by this.

HELENA
Oh, yes. Good acting. Show me puzzled looks,
I know you're winking when I turn my back!

She starts to leave.

LYSANDER
Stay, Helena! I love you. By my life, I do.

HELENA
Oh, yes, bravo!

HERMIA
Lysander, don't make fun.

DEMETRIUS (*to HELENA*)
I love you more than this man ever did!

LYSANDER
Oh yeah, you think? Let's see you prove it, kid!

> *The two men move to fight. HERMIA and HELENA try to pull them apart.*

HERMIA (*to HELENA*)
They're joking, right?

HELENA
Of course, and so are you!

LYSANDER (*to HERMIA*)
Get off of me, you fly, you cockroach. Shoo!

HERMIA (*to LYSANDER*)
Lysander, look, it's me. Your Hermia!
As fair now as I was an hour ago
When we both said "I love you" on the bank.
If this is all a joke, please stop it now.
(*realizing*) Oh, God… It's not a joke. You're leaving me.

LYSANDER
Not "leaving;" LEFT. I left you. We are done.
I've no desire to see you ever again.
Be certain, nothing truer, it's no joke
That I do hate you and love Helena.

HERMIA
O, me! (*to HELENA*) You juggler! You canker-blossom!
You thief of love! What, have you come by night
And stolen my love's heart from him?

HELENA
Good grief,
The joke goes on! Have you no modesty,
No maiden shame, no touch of bashfulness?
Fie, fie! You counterfeit, you puppet, you!

HERMIA
"Puppet?" Why so? Ah, that way goes the game.
Now I perceive that she has made compare
Between our statures. Look at how she stands!
And with her personage, her tall personage,
Her so-called "height," she has prevailed with him.
And have you grown so high in his esteem
Because I am so dwarfish and so low?
And how low am I, you painted maypole? Speak!
How low am I? I am not quite so low
That these nails cannot reach into your eyes!

HERMIA attacks.

HELENA
I pray you, though you mock me, gentlemen,
Don't let her strike me. You perhaps may think,
Because she is something lower than myself,
That I can match her.

HERMIA
Lower! There again!

They fight. HELENA puts HERMIA in a firm hold.

HELENA
All right! All right! I did it. I confess.

HERMIA
Confess to what?

HELENA
I told Demetrius
You would be here. So I could follow him.
Forgive me, Hermia: I've been such a fool.
I'll follow you no more, but let me go.

HERMIA
Well go, what's keeping you?

HELENA
I'm still in love.

HERMIA
With my Lysander?

HERMIA attacks again, and they fight more.

HELENA
No, Demetrius!

LYSANDER
Be not afraid! She will not harm you, Helena.

HELENA and HERMIA are pulled apart.

HELENA
She was a vixen when we went to school,
And though she may be little, she is fierce!

HERMIA
"Little" again! Nothing but "low" and "little."
She's asking for it! Do not hold me back!

LYSANDER
Be gone, you dwarf, you ant, you tiny speck!

HERMIA struggles against LYSANDER and falls to the ground.

DEMETRIUS
Don't bully her! You waste your breath
Defending Helen when she loves you not.

LYSANDER
Let's see you back your claims up with your fists.

DEMETRIUS
I'd love to.

LYSANDER
Good, then follow if you dare.

DEMETRIUS
"Follow?" Nay, I'll go with you, cheek by jowl.

Exit LYSANDER and DEMITRIUS.

HERMIA
Somehow you're at the root of this, I'm certain.
Give me a hand, please Helena.

HELENA
Nay, I'd rather use my legs to run away.

Exit.

HERMIA
I am amazed, and know not what to say.

Exit.

OBERON
This is your negligence! Again you failed!

PUCK
Believe me, king of shadows, I mistook!

OBERON
Were they mistakes or were they childish pranks?

PUCK
Did you not tell me I should know the John
By the Athenian garments he had on?
I have enchanted an Athenian's sight
Just as you asked me to, O Prince of Night.
Besides, I'm glad it all shook out this way
It's funny!

OBERON
Fix it.

PUCK
Yes, sir, right away!

OBERON
We know these lovers seek a place to fight.
Now I want you to overcast the night.
And lead these testy rivals so astray,
That one comes not within the other's way.

PUCK
For how long, sir?

OBERON
Until both men collapse,
Then: creep up to Lysander where he naps
And use this herb on him.

PUCK
What's this one for?

OBERON
To break the spell you placed on him before.

PUCK
My fairy lord, this whole thing sounds like fun!

OBERON
No. Don't make this a game. Just get it done.

Exit OBERON.

PUCK
Up and down,
Up and down,
I will lead them up and down
I am feared in field and town,
Goblin lead them up and down.

Enter LYSANDER with a sharp stick.

LYSANDER
Where are you, proud Demetrius? Speak up!

PUCK
Here, villain, drawn and ready. Where are you?

LYSANDER.
I'm not sure. It's dark. But I'll find you soon enough!

PUCK
Follow me, then. This way!

Exit LYSANDER. Enter DEMETRIUS.

DEMETRIUS
Where are you hiding from me, cowardly Lysander? Here, in this bush? (*He attacks the bush. There's no one in it.*) Nay. Show yourself!

PUCK
I see you, little bush-whacker. Come, must you keep hedging, or will you fight me like a man?

DEMETRIUS
I'll fight you if you tell me where you are.

PUCK
Follow my voice!

Exit DEMETRIUS. Re-enter LYSANDER.

LYSANDER
He runs ahead of me and dares me on.
But when I get to where he is, he's gone.
Too dark to fight. I'll rest here till the dawn.

He sleeps. Re-enter DEMETRIUS and PUCK.

PUCK
Ho, ho, you coward! Won't you come and fight?

DEMETRIUS
If you would show your face to me, I might!
Where are you now?

PUCK
Come hither. I am there.

DEMETRIUS
No, you're just mocking me. This isn't fair.
Watch out for me, Lysander, come sunrise.
Till then, I think I might just shut my eyes.

He sleeps. Enter HELENA.

HELENA
O weary night, O long and tedious night.

She sleeps.

PUCK
Yet but three? Come one more.
Two of both kinds make up four.

Enter HERMIA.

HERMIA
Never so weary, never so in woe.
I can no further crawl, no further go.

She sleeps.

PUCK
On the ground, sleep sound.
(*to LYSANDER*)
When you wake, you shall take
True delight in the sight
Of your former lady's eye.
Jack shall have Jill, Nought shall go ill,
And all shall be well.

Exit.

ACT 4, SCENE 1

The wood. The sleepers remain.

Enter TITANIA, BOTTOM, FAIRIES, and OBERON, who watches from afar.

TITANIA
Come, love, sit down upon this flowery bed,
While I stick roses round your sleek, smooth head,
And kiss your fair large ears, my gentle joy.

BOTTOM
Where's Peaseblossom?

PEASEBLOSSOM
Ready.

BOTTOM
Scratch my head, Peaseblossom. Where's Doctor Cobweb?

COBWEB
Ready.

BOTTOM
Cobweb, can you recommend a good barber around here? Methinks I am marvelous hairy about the face, and frankly it itches a lot.

The FAIRIES giggle.

BOTTOM
Or you could just help Peaseblossom to scratch.

TITANIA
My love, what do you desire to eat?

BOTTOM
For some reason I have a great desire to eat a bale of hay. Good hay, sweet hay, has no fellow.

TITANIA
I have a venturous fairy that shall seek some out.

MOTE
Pick me!

FAIRIES
No, me! No, me!

BOTTOM
Yes, but I pray you, let none of your people stir me. I feel a nap coming. Yep, here it is.

TITANIA
Sleep, dear, and I will wind you in my arms.
Fairies, be gone. And be always away.

Exeunt FAIRIES.

TITANIA
So does the woodbine gently curl around
The honeysuckle and the barky elm.
O, how I love thee! How I dote on thee!

They sleep. Enter PUCK.

OBERON
Welcome, good Puck. Look at this sweet sight. I'd thought it would amuse me, but instead I'm filled with pity. Before you arrived I taunted her, and she didn't fight back. Just said, "I beg your pardon, sir," and smiled, and placed another flower in the monster's hairy temple. I will undo this hateful imperfection of her eyes. And Puck, while you're at it, take the donkey head off of that guy. Send him back to Athens where he belongs.

PUCK
Yes, sir.

OBERON
But first I will release the fairy queen.
(*To TITANIA*)
Be the one you used to be.
See things as you used to see.
Now, my Titania, wake you, my sweet queen.

TITANIA
My Oberon! What visions have I seen!
Methought I was enamored of an ass.

OBERON
There lies your love.

TITANIA
How came these things to pass?
Oh, how my eyes do loathe his hairy face!

OBERON
Let's have some music, shall we? There, that's good.
Puck, go to. Come, my queen, take hands with me.
And rock the ground whereon these sleepers be.

OBERON and TITANIA dance away.

Enter THESEUS, HIPPOLYTA, and EGEUS.

HIPPOLYTA
Dear Theseus, look!

THESEUS
How odd! What nymphs are these?

EGEUS
My lord, this is my daughter here asleep.
And that's Lysander. And Demetrius, there!
And this is Helena, my daughter's friend.
I wonder why they're all together here…

THESEUS blows his hunting horn and the lovers wake up.

THESEUS
Good morning, friends. I pray you all, stand up.
You men, I thought you two were enemies.
And here I find you dreaming side by side.

LYSANDER
My lord, I must reply amazedly,
Half sleep, half waking: but as yet, I swear,
I cannot truly say how I came here.

EGEUS
Enough! Enough, my lord. We've heard enough.
I beg the law, the law, upon his head.
It's clear they planned to run away from us,
To leave Demetrius without a bride,
And me without a heed to my consent!

DEMETRIUS
My lord, fair Helen told me of this plan,
And I in fury followed to this wood.
It's all a blur. I know not by what power,
But in the night, my love to Hermia
Melted as the snow. And now the jewel,
The apple and the pleasure of my eye
Is only Helena. To her, my lord,
I must be wed. To her I must be true.

THESEUS
Well, that falls out quite nicely, doesn't it?

HIPPOLYTA
I want the longer version of this tale.

THESEUS
Egeus, sorry, you've been overruled.
But to the temple I invite you come,
For there, three couples shall be wed this day.

    Gasps of astonishment and joy.

THESEUS
Aye, this one, that one, and that one. You see?
Away with us to Athens, three and three!
Come, Hippolyta.

    Exeunt THESEUS, HIPPOLYTA, and EGEUS.

DEMETRIUS
It seems unreal.

HERMIA
I know. I feel as though
I'm seeing the world through out-of-focus eyes.

HELENA (*to DEMETRIUS*)
You came to me like treasure in the sand,
My own, and not my own.

DEMETRIUS
Are you sure that we are awake? It seems to me that this is all a dream.
And... wait... was not the duke just here?

HERMIA
Yes, and my father.

HELENA
And Hippolyta.

LYSANDER
And we're to follow them.

DEMETRIUS
Why, then, we are awake! Let's follow on,
And on the way, we can recount our dreams.

Exeunt lovers. BOTTOM wakes up.

BOTTOM
When my cue comes, call me. I think the line is "Most fair Pyramus," isn't that right, Peter Quince? Peter Quince? Yoo hoo. Flute the bellows-maker? Snout the tinker? Starveling? Did they leave me here asleep? I have had a most rare vision. I have had a dream—though no man can say what my dream was. I dreamt I was... I dreamt I had... but I'd sound foolish saying what I dreamt I had. The eye of man has not heard, the ear of man has not seen, man's hand is not able to taste, nor his heart to report what my dream was. I will get Peter Quince to write a ballad of this dream. And it will be called "Bottom's Dream." And I shall sing it for the duke during intermission. Or better yet, I'll sing it when Thisbe dies.

Exit.

ACT 4, SCENE 2

Athens, behind Quince's house.

Enter QUINCE, FLUTE, SNOUT, and STARVELING.

QUINCE
Have you called at Bottom's house? Is he there?

STARVELING
No one's seen him.

SNOUT
It's as we'd thought. He's been transported.

FLUTE
Do you think we could go on without him?

QUINCE
There's no way. There's not a man in Athens can play Pyramus like he can.

SNOUT
He had the sharpest wit of any handicraft man I ever knew.

STARVELING
And the handsomest face.

FLUTE
I miss his sweet voice.

    Enter SNUG.

SNUG
Masters, I just saw the duke coming from the temple with a great crowd behind him. Look! If only the play weren't canceled, we'd have all been made men!

STARVELING
O poor us! O poor Bottom!

    Enter BOTTOM.

BOTTOM
Where are these lads? Where are these hearts?

QUINCE
Bottom! O most courageous day! O most happy hour!

BOTTOM

Masters, I'm sure you're wondering what happened to me, and I will tell you everything, but not now, for time is of the eminence. Let's to the palace. For tonight, we open!

Exeunt with cheers.

ACT 5, SCENE 1

Athens. The palace of THESEUS.

Enter THESEUS, HIPPOLYTA, and PHILOSTRATE.

HIPPOLYTA
It's strange, my dear, the tale these lovers tell.

THESEUS
More strange than true: and harder to believe,
Especially the part about the fairies.
Lovers and madmen have such seething brains.

HIPPOLYTA
Their visions were remarkable, for sure,
And yet their stories showed a constancy
That made me question whether they are mad.
Perhaps there's more truth here than we perceive.

Enter LYSANDER, DEMETRIUS, HERMIA, and HELENA.

THESEUS
And look at that! Here come the lovers now.
My gentle friends, I wish you joy this day,
And more in all the days ahead.

LYSANDER
Good duke,
These wishes we return a thousand-fold.

THESEUS
Oh, Philostrate!

PHILOSTRATE
Here, mighty Theseus!

THESEUS
What entertainments are in store tonight?

PHILOSTRATE
Oh, many, sir. I've got the list right here.

THESEUS
Well, read them out.

PHILOSTRATE (*reads*)
"The battle with the Centaurs, to be sung
By an Athenian eunuch to the harp."

THESEUS
No. We'll have none of that.

PHILOSTRATE
"The riot of the tipsy Bacchanals,
Tearing the Thracian singer in their rage."

THESEUS
Already seen it. Next.

PHILOSTRATE
"A tedious, brief scene of young Pyramus
And his love, Thisbe: Very tragical, with laughs."

THESEUS
Funny and tragical! This sounds like one to see. So it's a play?

PHILOSTRATE
A play, my lord, some seven minutes long.

THESEUS
Who's in it?

PHILOSTRATE
Hard-handed men who work in Athens here.
They've labored with their hands for many years,
But never with their minds that much till now.

THESEUS
They sound delightful.

PHILOSTRATE
No, my noble lord;
This play is not for you: I've seen it done.
The casting makes no sense. The script is worse.

HIPPOLYTA
But is it funny?

PHILOSTRATE
It is funny, yes.
Though never in the way that they intend.

THESEUS
I'll see that play. For nothing can go wrong
When simpleness and duty rule the day.
Go, bring them in.

PHILOSTRATE
Hey! You guys are on!

QUINCE
We are?

PHILOSTRATE
So please your grace, the Prologue will begin.

THESEUS
Let him approach.

Enter QUINCE as Prologue.

QUINCE
If we offend, it is with our good will.
That you should think, we come not to offend,
But with good will. To show our simple skill,
That is the true beginning of our end.
The actors are at hand and by their show
You shall know all that you are like to know.

Exit.

THESEUS
Oh wow. That speech was like a tangled chain.

Enter SNOUT as Wall.

SNOUT
In this same interlude it doth befall
That I, one Snout by name, present a wall;
And such a wall, as I would have you think,
That had in it a crannied hole or chink,
Through which two lovers, Pyramus and Thisbe,
Did whisper often very secretly.
This piece of plaster in my hand doth show
That I am that same wall; the truth is so!
And this the cranny is, right and sinister,
Through which the fearful lovers are to whisper.

THESEUS
That is the most talkative wall I have ever seen.

SNOUT
Shhh! Here comes Pyramus.

Enter BOTTOM as Pyramus.

BOTTOM
O grim-look'd night! O night with hue so black!
O night, which ever art when day is not!
O night, O night! alack, alack, alack,
I fear my Thisbe's promise is forgot!
And thou, O wall, O sweet, O lovely wall,
That stands between her father's ground and mine!
Thou wall, O wall, O sweet and lovely wall,
Show me thy chink, to blink through with mine eyne!

Wall holds up his fingers.

BOTTOM
Thanks, courteous wall: Jove shield thee well for this!
But what see I? No Thisbe do I see.
O wicked wall, through whom I see no bliss!
Cursed be thy stones for thus deceiving me!

Enter FLUTE, as Thisbe, pushed by QUINCE.

QUINCE
Get out there, you're missing your cue!

FLUTE
O wall, full often hast thou heard my moans,
For parting my fair Pyramus and me!
My cherry lips have often kissed thy stones,
Thy stones with lime and hair knit up in thee.

BOTTOM
I see a voice: now will I to the chink,
To spy and I can hear my Thisbe's face. Thisbe!

FLUTE
My love thou art, my love I think.

BOTTOM
O kiss me through the hole of this vile wall!

FLUTE
I kiss the wall's hole, not your lips at all.

BOTTOM
Wilt thou at Ninny's tomb meet me straightway?

FLUTE
Of course I shall! I come without delay.

Exeunt Pyramus and Thisbe.

SNOUT
Thus have I, Wall, my part discharged so.
And, being done, thus Wall away doth go.

Exit.

THESEUS
There goes the wall.

HIPPOLYTA
Ooh, and here comes a noble beast.

Enter SNUG as Lion and STARVELING as Moonshine.

SNUG
You ladies, you, whose gentle hearts do fear
The smallest monstrous mouse that creeps on floor,
May now perchance both quake and tremble here,
When lion rough in wildest rage doth roar.
Then know that I am Snug the joiner, see?
(*He pulls up his mask.*)
And not a lion as I seem to be.

THESEUS
He seems like a very gentle beast.

STARVELING
This lantern doth the silvery moon present…

EGEUS
It looks like that moon wanes a bit.

THESEUS
Haha! Good one.

STARVELING
This lantern doth the horned moon present;
Myself the man in the moon do seem to be.

THESEUS
If that's true, shouldn't he be inside the lantern?

HIPPOLYTA
I am aweary of this moon: would he would change!

The audience laughs.

AUDIENCE
Change! Change!

STARVELING (*frustrated and upset*)
Look, all I have to say, is, to tell you that the lantern is the moon; I, the man in the
moon; this thorn bush, my thorn bush; and this dog, my dog.

THESEUS
I think we hurt his feelings. Sorry, moon!

HIPPOLYTA
Shhh! Here comes Thisbe.

Enter Thisbe.

FLUTE
This is old Ninny's tomb. Where is my love?

SNUG
Roooar.

FLUTE
Oh!

Thisbe runs off, accidentally dropping her mantle.

EGEUS
Well roared, Lion!

THESEUS
Well run, Thisbe.

HIPPOLYTA
Well shone, Moon.

Re-enter Prologue.

QUINCE (*indicating the mantle*)
And, as she fled, her mantle she let fall,
Which Lion vile, with bloody mouth, did stain.

Lion takes the mantle in his teeth and shakes it, then leaves it there.

Exit Lion.

QUINCE
Along comes Pyramus!

Enter Pyramus.

Exit Prologue.

BOTTOM
Sweet Moon, I thank thee for thy sunny beams;
For, by thy gracious, golden, glittering gleams,
I trust to take of truest Thisbe sight.
But stay, O spite!
What dreadful dole is here!
Eyes, do you see?
How can it be?
O dainty duck! O dear!
Thy mantle good,
What, stained with blood?

HIPPOLYTA
This is tragic.

BOTTOM
O why could not this lion have been tame?
This lion vile, he hath deflowered my dear:
Who is—no, no—who was the fairest dame
That lived, that loved, that liked, that looked with cheer.
Come, tears, confound;
Out, sword, and wound
The pap of Pyramus;
Ay, that left pap,
Where heart doth hop.
(*Stabbing himself*)
Thus die I! Thus, thus, thus.
Now am I dead,
Now am I fled;

My soul is in the sky:
Tongue, lose thy light;
Moon, take thy flight:

Exit Moonshine.

BOTTOM
Now die, die, die, die, die.

He dies.

HIPPOLYTA
Is he dead?

THESEUS
Looks that way. But with the help of a surgeon he might yet recover.

Re-enter Thisbe.

FLUTE
Asleep, my love? What, dead, my dove?
O Pyramus, arise!
Speak, speak. Quite dumb? Dead, dead? A tomb
Must cover thy sweet eyes.
These lily lips, this cherry nose,
These yellow cowslip cheeks,
Are gone, are gone. Lovers, make moan.
His eyes were green as leeks.
Tongue, not a word. Come, trusty sword.
Come, blade, my breast imbrue. (*Stabs herself*)
And, farewell, friends. Thus Thisbe ends.
Adieu, adieu, adieu.

She dies.

THESEUS
So Moonshine and Lion are left to bury the dead.

HIPPOLYTA
Well, don't forget the wall.

BOTTOM
Actually, the wall that parted their father's houses is gone. We cover that in the epilogue. Would you like to hear the epilogue?

THESEUS
No epilogue, I pray you; for your play needs no excuse. This was a fine tragedy, and very well discharged. Now, what's next?

SNOUT
There's also a dance.

THESEUS
Well, let's see that!

> *They dance.*

> *Exeunt.*

> *Enter PUCK.*

PUCK
If we shadows have offended,
Think but this, and all is mended,
That you have but slumbered here
While these visions did appear.
And this weak and idle theme,
Yielding no more than a dream,
Gentles, do not reprehend:
If you pardon, we will mend.

CURTAIN

ABOUT LIGHTHOUSE

Lighthouse Plays was founded to address a recurring challenge for theater directors and educators: finding high-quality scripts for young people.

We have found that most scripts created for kids are overly simplistic, bordering on patronizing. The stakes are minimal, the characters lack depth, and the presumption is clear — kids have insufficient acting ability, so the scripts need to be foolproof.

At Lighthouse Plays, we think about kids differently. We believe that with the right material and the right direction, kids can be held to a higher standard and produce theater that has a powerful effect on audiences.

Check out **lighthouseplays.com** to see our full library of plays,

from *The Odyssey* to *Alice in Wonderland* and more!

Book design by Laura Wimer: **iamlew.com**

Cover illustrations by Kate Zaremba: **katezarembacompany.com**

Published in partnership with Can't Not: **cantnotproductions.com**

Made in the USA
San Bernardino, CA
11 May 2018